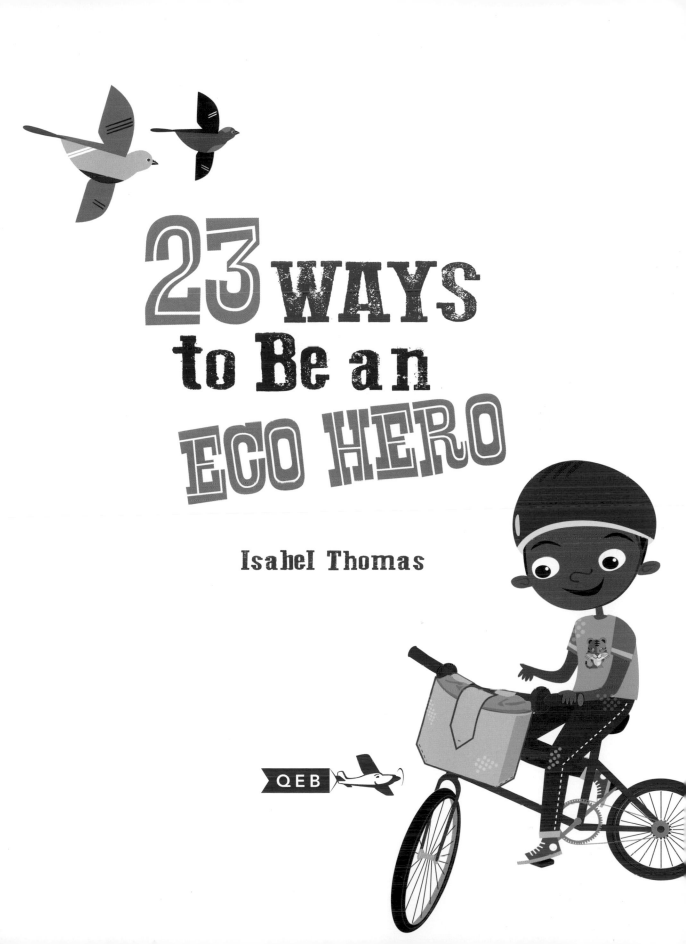

23 WAYS to Be an ECO HERO

Isabel Thomas

QEB

Written by Isabel Thomas • Illustrated by Chris Andrews
Managing Editor: Laura Knowles
Designer: Julie Francis
Art Director: Susi Martin
Publisher: Zeta Jones
Associate Publisher: Maxime Boucknooghe
Production: Nikki Ingram

First published in the UK in 2015 by QED Publishing

Publishied in the United States in 2015 by
QEB Publishing, Inc.
6 Orchard, Lake Forest, CA 92630

A CIP record for this book is available from the Library of Congress.

ISBN 978 1 60992 921 3

Originated in Hong Kong by Cypress Colours (HK) Ltd
Printed and bound in China
by 1010 Printing International Ltd

10 9 8 7 6 5 4 3 2 1   15 16 17 18 19

NOTE TO PARENTS

The projects in this book are of varying levels of difficulty, and many require the use of tools. They are designed to be constructed with adult help, and not for the child to make on his or her own.

Children should be supervised at all times when using potentially dangerous equipment.

The author and publisher accept no liability for any injuries sustained in making these projects, which are undertaken entirely at your own risk.

Contents

Have You Ever Dreamed of Being a Hero?

Get ready. The planet's under threat and it's time for you to come to the rescue!

Earth isn't about to be zapped by a giant laser or conquered by aliens. It's much worse than that. The planet is being damaged by the everyday actions of more than 7 billion people who call it home.

Most of us don't even realize we're doing anything wrong. Does it really matter if one person drops one empty bag on the ground? But tiny actions add up. If 7 billion people drop an empty bag, that's enough litter to stretch to the Moon and back. Twice.

Luckily, small eco-friendly actions can add up too—and that's where you come in. You don't have to be super strong, super smart, or wear your pants over your tights to be an eco hero. (Phew!) You just need to find ways to make a difference in your local area. The projects in this book are the perfect way to start.

Change Champion

BE A CHANGE CHAMPION—You have even more impact if you get other people involved. The Change Champion boxes are packed with ideas to help you shout about your actions, and turn your whole community into eco heroes!

How to Use This Book

The projects in this book are grouped into three categories. If it's spring or summer, try transforming your back garden with a bunch of Wildlife Warrior projects. If it's raining outside, get creative indoors and become a Waste Zapper. The last batch of projects will help transform your whole household into a Green Machine.

WILDLIFE WARRIOR

Turn any outdoor area into a wildlife haven, with projects that create food, water, and shelter for plants and animals.

WASTE ZAPPER

Declare war on waste! These projects will help you reuse and recycle, by giving your trash a second life.

GREEN MACHINE

Join the green team with projects that show you and your family how to reduce waste and use less energy.

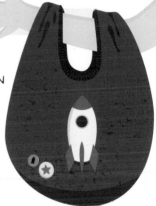

HOW TO SAVE THE WORLD SAFELY

You're never too young to be an eco hero, but sometimes you will need help from an adult. Before starting each project, read the instructions carefully with an adult. Make sure you will have an adult to help you with tricky steps before you get started.

Ask an Adult

Look out for this icon. It tells you which steps are only suitable for an adult to do.

Plant a Pond

Making a mini pond is as easy as planting a tree. You don't need a huge garden, or special equipment. Just recycle anything that holds water, from a trash-can lid to an old sled!

you will need

- trash-can lid, dishpan, or another old, waterproof container (ideally at least 16 inches wide and 10 inches deep)
- gravel
- flat stones (such as broken paving stones)
- a few large stones, bricks, or pebbles
- two or three water plants
- rainwater

tools

- shovel or trowel
- spirit level

* If you don't have ground that you can dig, place your container on a patio or balcony, and go straight to step 5.

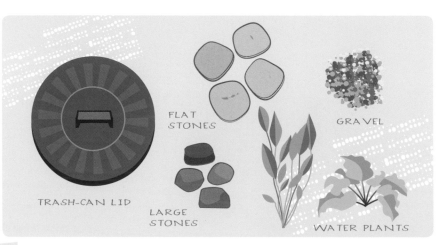

FLAT STONES

GRAVEL

TRASH-CAN LID

LARGE STONES

WATER PLANTS

1. Choose a spot that gets a mixture of sun and shade during the day. Put the container on the ground, and use the trowel to mark around the edge.

* Make sure your mini pond does not get too much sun, or the water will evaporate.

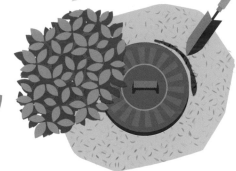

2. Dig a hole as deep as the container. Keep the soil for step 3. When you put the container in the hole, the top should be level with the ground. Use a spirit level to make sure the container is not tilted.

6

TAKING GARE OF YOUR POND

Wildlife needs water to survive, and even a tiny pond will bring birds, insects, and other animals to your garden. Once the pond has settled, minibeasts will be the first to move in. Birds, frogs, toads, and mammals will visit to drink, bathe, and feast on the insect inhabitants!

Add plants to keep your pond fresh and healthy. Choose at least one plant that adds oxygen to the water and one plant that grows on the surface. Tuck the roots into the gravel, or simply place pots on the bottom of your pond. Make sure you keep it filled up with water.

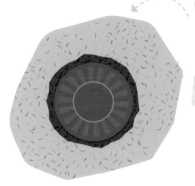

3. Scoop soil back into the gaps around the sides of the container.

4. Arrange flat stones around the edge of the pond. They will hold the container in place and stop soil from washing into the pond when it rains.

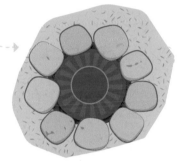

* Use rainwater to fill and top off your pond. The Let It Rain project on page 18 will help you to gather enough rainwater.

5. Cover the bottom of the container with a layer of gravel.

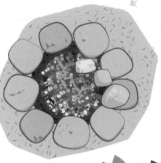

6. Add some large stones or pebbles. A tall pile on one side will help animals to climb in and out.

7. Fill the pond with water, and wait for wildlife to arrive!

* A pile of logs near your pond will help to attract frogs and toads, who love to hide! If you don't have logs, make a frog shelter by burying a flowerpot on its side.

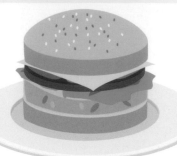

Eco-Burgers

Just one meat-free day every week can reduce your family's carbon footprint. Cook these beautiful bean burgers to help convince everyone that meat-free meals are just as scrumptious.

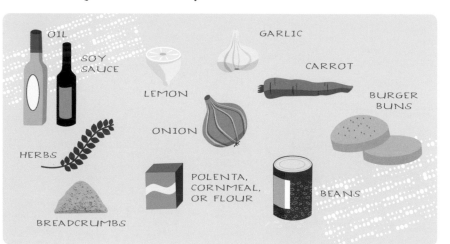

OIL
SOY SAUCE
GARLIC
CARROT
LEMON
ONION
BURGER BUNS
HERBS
POLENTA, CORNMEAL, OR FLOUR
BEANS
BREADCRUMBS

you will need

- 5 tablespoons oil
- one onion, diced
- one garlic clove, chopped
- one carrot
- two 14-ounce cans of butter beans, soybeans, kidney beans, or cannellini beans
- handful of fresh herbs
- 2 handfuls of breadcrumbs
- one tablespoon soy sauce
- juice of ½ a lemon
- handful of polenta, cornmeal, or flour
- 4 burger buns

tools

- large bowl
- potato masher or fork
- grater

1. Ask an adult to heat a tablespoon of oil in a frying pan, and cook the chopped onion and garlic for 5 minutes.

2. Grate the carrot and add it to the pan. Cook gently for 5 minutes until the vegetables are soft, and take them off the heat.

Ask an Adult

* Ask an adult to help you chop the onion and garlic before you get started.

3. While the vegetables cool, drain and rinse the beans. Tip them into a large bowl, and mash with a fork or potato masher.

GOBBLING UP RESOURCES

Meat is expensive to buy for a good reason—animal farms use huge amounts of land, water, and energy. Every year, 65 billion animals are farmed for food. They gobble down almost a third of the world's crops, but only a small proportion of the protein and energy in their feed is passed on to people in meat, milk, and eggs. It would be much more energy efficient to grow crops to feed people directly.

4. Add the cooled vegetables to the bowl. Tip in the breadcrumbs, chopped herbs, soy sauce, and lemon juice too.

* Make breadcrumbs by grating a chunk of stale bread, or a spare burger bun! You could use two large spoonfuls of mashed potato instead.

5. Use your hands to squish and mix all the ingredients together.

6. When everything is well mixed, divide the mixture into six. Shape each piece into a patty and roll it in the polenta, cornmeal, or flour.

Change Champion

Red meat has the worst impact on the environment. Raising cattle uses 28 times more land and 11 times more water than raising poultry. Cattle burps are an even bigger problem. Microbes inside their stomachs help cattle to digest tough food, such as grass. These microbes produce methane, a greenhouse gas that is a major cause of global warming. This makes meat-free meals one of the top ways for an eco hero to tackle global warming.

Ask an Adult

7. Ask an adult to heat a few tablespoons of oil in the frying pan. Fry the burgers for 5 minutes on each side, until they are golden and crispy.

Yum Yum!

8. Serve the burgers in buns, with your favorite toppings.

Bag It Up

Throwaway plastic bags are an eco-disaster. It's so easy to help—just take your own bag when you go shopping. Earn extra eco-hero points if you make your own. Here are two ways to turn old clothes into a brand new bag—no sewing needed!

you will need

- old T-shirt or vest top, made of stretchy fabric

tools

- sharp fabric scissors
- bowl
- pen

OLD T-SHIRT

1. Turn the T-shirt or top inside out, and carefully cut off each sleeve.

* **Don't cut the seams off—they'll form the strong straps of your bag!**

* **This is a great way to recycle a favorite T-shirt or sports top that you've outgrown but can't bear to throw away!**

2. Fold the T-shirt in half lengthwise. Position the bowl so it overlaps the folded corner, and draw around it.

4. Unfold the T-shirt, and draw a line across the bottom, around 2 inches from the hem.

2 in.

3. Use scissors to cut neatly along the line. This shape will be the opening of your bag.

Ask an Adult

5. Working from the bottom of the T-shirt, cut along each side seam, stopping when you get to the line.

6. Now place the scissors around 1 inch from the left-hand seam, and cut through both layers of the T-shirt, stopping when you get to the line.

1 in.

7. Tie the two strips of fabric together with a tight knot.

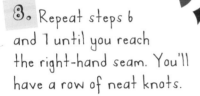

8. Repeat steps 6 and 7 until you reach the right-hand seam. You'll have a row of neat knots.

9. Working from the left-hand seam, grab the loose ends of two adjacent knots. Tie them together. Repeat with the next pair of knots until you reach the right-hand seam.

THE PLASTIC PROBLEM

Around the world, a million plastic bags are handed out every minute. The average American family takes home almost 1,500 plastic shopping bags a year, and less than 5 percent are recycled.

Making plastic uses up vital resources, with 12 million barrels of oil used for plastic bags each year. The pollution it causes is an even bigger problem. Plastic litters the oceans and is a threat to wildlife, and plastic bags can take up to 1,000 years to break down.

10. Turn the T-shirt right side out again. This will hide the ends of each knot.

Change Champion

Plastic bags can be reused, but they are often too thin to last long. A reusable fabric bag is much stronger, and looks better too.

11. Your bag is ready to use. Stuff it into a backpack or coat pocket, ready for eco-hero action when a shop assistant says...

"Would you like a bag?"

Jeans Bag

Reusing old clothes is a great way to be an eco hero. If you have a sewing machine handy, you can turn an old pillowcase, duvet, or curtains into stylish bags for your books or supplies. For special occasions, transform an old pair of jeans into a slouchy shoulder bag.

OLD PAIR OF JEANS OR PANTS

2 OLD SCARVES OR LONG SCRAPS OF FABRIC

you will need

- pair of old pants or jeans (with belt loops)
- 2 old scarves or long scraps of fabric
- needle, thread, and old button (optional)

tools

- sharp fabric scissors

1. Turn the jeans or pants inside-out.

2. Tie a large knot in each leg, as close to the top of the leg as possible.

* Pull the knots really tight!

3. Trim the bottom of each leg off, about 2 inches from the knot.

2 in.

* Denim jeans are great for this project, as they'll make a tough, long-lasting bag.

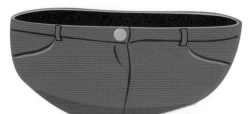

4. Turn the pants the right way around again—you've made the shell of your bag.

* Really push out the corners to give it shape.

12

Change Champion

Cotton is the fiber used to make almost half of our clothes, including denim. It is farmed on huge plantations, gobbling land, energy, and water. More resources are used up taking the cotton to factories, turning it into clothes, and shipping them to stores. Old clothes can be recycled—even grubby, worn-out textiles can be turned into stuffing for cushions and sofas. But reusing clothes is better for the environment. When you grow out of clothes, be an eco hero by donating them to friends or family, charity shops, or clothing banks—or find clever ways to turn them into something new, rather than hitting the shops. Remember to swap and shop secondhand yourself.

5. Add a handle to the front of the bag by tying a scarf or long scrap of fabric between two of the belt loops.

6. Flip the bag over, and repeat step 5 on the back to add a second strap.

7. Your bag is ready to use! Add badges, brooches, or key rings for extra sparkle, or make a matching flower decoration with the scraps of leftover fabric.

More Ideas

• To make a fabric flower, cut three flower shapes in different sizes. Layer and sew together with a contrasting button at the center. Ten loops of thread should do the trick.

Super Stool

Stiff, strong, and light—corrugated cardboard is the perfect packing material. Every year, enough is made to cover Iceland, twice! Luckily, it's one of the easiest materials to reuse and recycle. Follow these steps to see a box morph into furniture fit for a hero.

DUCT TAPE

LARGE CARDBOARD BOX

you will need

- large, corrugated cardboard box (square is ideal)
- duct tape
- two bolts or screws (optional)
- old comics or magazines, plus PVA glue (optional)

tools

- small saw
- scissors
- ruler/set square
- pen or pencil

* Corrugated cardboard is one of the best materials to recycle at home. It's tough, but easy to cut, fold, and decorate. Collect empty boxes and cartons from stores and garden centers, and design your own furniture, decorations, and even toys.

1. Cut the lid off the box, and tape the flaps at the bottom together.

Ask an Adult

2. Cut along each corner fold, and let the sides flop down to give you a flat piece of cardboard in the shape of a "+."

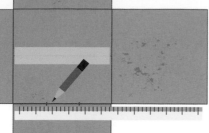

3. Choose one flap to work on first. Use the ruler to measure ⅓ and ⅔ of the way along the fold. Mark each point with a cross.

4. Use a ruler or set square and a pen to score a line from each cross, down to the bottom of the flap. Press hard enough to mark a groove in the surface of the cardboard.

5. Cut along the fold from either edge, stopping when you get to the crosses.

6. Bring the outer edges together to make a triangle. The scored lines will make it easy to fold the cardboard. Use a strip of duct tape to stick the edges together where they meet.

7. Repeat steps 3 to 6 with the other three flaps. You have made the legs of your chair.

15

8. Draw a line across each corner of the base, from the edge of one leg to the next. Score along the lines.

9. Fold each leg upward, and use duct tape to hold them in place.

10. Now fold in the corners, holding them in place with more duct tape.

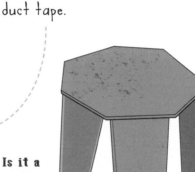

* Is it a stool? Is it a table? You choose! You could add decoration, or follow steps 11 to 14 to change your design into a chair.

COOL CARDBOARD

A typical person throws away two trees' worth of paper and cardboard every year. Reusing cardboard means less trash is burned or buried as landfill.

Most corrugated cardboard is made from fast-growing pine trees. They are pulped and made into sheets of brown paper, which is glued together on huge machines. The trees are renewable, but the energy used to make the cardboard and ship it around the world is not. Save energy by reusing and recycling boxes.

Making the back

11. To make a chair back, you'll need a sheet of cardboard roughly the same size as the seat. Cut two corners off to make an arch shape.

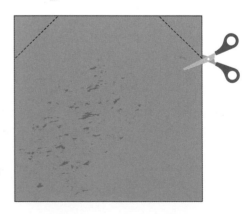

12. Draw and score a line about a third of the way up. Next use a ruler and set square to divide the bottom into thirds. Cut along the lines, up to the score.

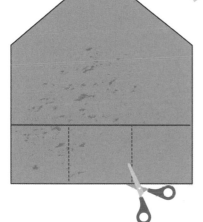

13. Cut the corners off the outer thirds, as shown, then bend them back at the scored line.

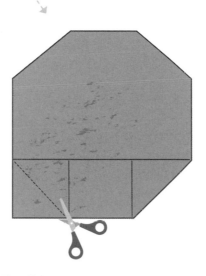

14. Slide the middle third between the two layers of cardboard that make up the back of your stool. Pull the outer thirds together, bending the back into a curved shape. Use screws or bolts to join all the layers together.

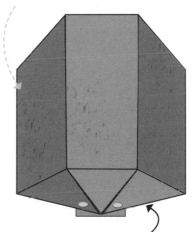

* Use the bolts to secure the back to the seat and use extra tape to smooth over the edges.

Adding Style

If you don't like the eco-chic cardboard look, decorate your stool or table using one of these ideas.

- Chop up cartoon strips from an old comic or magazine. Stick them all over the chair using PVA glue. Brush with watered-down PVA glue to seal your superhero design.

- Ask your friends to graffiti their names and messages all over your new piece of furniture.

- Cut a piece of foam to fit the top. Cover with a length of leftover fabric, and use a staple gun to fix your comfy cushion in place.

Let It Rain

When is a plastic bottle not an eco baddie? When it's transformed into a mini rain barrel! This project will help you collect enough rainwater to give houseplants a regular drink.

PEBBLES OR STONES

SUPERGLUE

PLASTIC BOTTLES

you will need

- old plastic bottles, any size or color
- waterproof paint or pens (optional)
- superglue
- large, clean pebbles or stones

tools

- scissors
- pen

A FREE DRINK!

Houseplants share your home, but they don't need to share your water supply. Watering plants with rainwater is better for the planet AND the plants, especially if the water in your house is softened.

Ask an Adult

1. Draw a line around the center of the bottle. Ask an adult to carefully cut it in half for you.

2. Turn the top half of the bottle upside down and make four marks at equal distances around the edge (like the points on a compass).

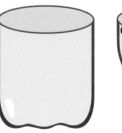

3. Draw a deep triangle between each pair of marks.

4. Cut out the four triangle shapes.

* The scraps of plastic can go in the recycling bin.

5. Now cut a straight line down from the point of each triangle toward the neck of the bottle, stopping just before you get to the bottom.

6. Fold out the four shapes, like the petals of a flower. Curve the tip of each one upward to make a bowl shape at the base of the petal. You can decorate the back of each petal using waterproof paints or pens.

7. Add some heavy stones to the bottom half of the bottle, then run the glue around the rim.

Don't drink the rainwater that collects in your mini rain barrel.

* Use the top parts of the collectors on their own, to brighten up patio containers.

8. Stick the plastic flower to the rim of the bottle. When the glue has dried, place the bottle on a garden table, wall, or patio, ready to collect rain!

Change Champion

These mini water collectors are perfect for a small patio or balcony. If you have a larger outdoor space, ask your family to invest in a rain barrel. These are large plastic barrels that store the rainwater that runs off the roof of a house, garage, or greenhouse. Water collected during the wet winter months can be used to water a garden (and houseplants) in the summer.

Batty Box

you will need

- 3 planks of rough, untreated wood, 20 x 6 inches in size and ½ to 1 inch thick
- eight 2-inch nails or eight 2-inch self-tapping screws
- water-based exterior paint, in a dark color

tools

- ruler and pencil
- saw
- hammer or screwdriver
- paintbrush

* Always use wood that has a rough-sawn finish and has not been treated with any chemicals. Chemicals harm bats.

* Make sure to get permission from an adult before starting this project. In some areas, it is illegal to open or remove a bat box once it is up, so check the law in your area.

If you're lucky, you may spot bats visiting your wildlife-friendly backyard at sunset. Give them a place to shelter and hibernate by building a bat roost.

PLANKS OF WOOD   PAINT   NAILS

1. Saw a quarter (5 in.) off the end of two of your planks of wood, so they now measure 15 inches long.

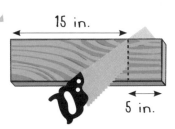

15 in.

5 in.

Ask an Adult

1 in. →

2. On one of these 15-inch lengths of wood, measure and mark two strips, each 1 inch wide. Ask an adult to help you saw the strips.

1/2 in. →

3. Use the ruler and pencil to mark a series of lines 1/2 inch apart, on the longest plank. Carefully saw into these by 1/16 inch, to make a ladder for bats to grip.

4. Drill two holes about 1 inch from the top.

5. You are ready to start assembling your bat roost. Make a sandwich with the long length of wood at the bottom, the two strips in the middle, and the short length on top.

6. Ask an adult to help you nail or screw the sandwich together. This will leave an entrance slit about 1 inch wide.

Entrance slit

7. Take one of the quarter pieces cut earlier, and nail or screw it to the end of the sandwich. This will be the roof. Make sure there are no gaps between the top and sides. Bats hate cold drafts!

Ask an Adult

* Never open the bat box once it is up. Instead, look and listen for signs that bats have moved in! You might see droppings on the bat ladder, or hear chattering sounds in the evenings.

8. Paint the box with two coats of water-based, non-toxic paint. Cover every part that will be exposed to weather, but don't paint the insides. A dark color such as black is best.

9. Ask an adult to help you hang your bat box 4 to 5 yards off the ground, in a sunny spot on a building or a strong tree.

* Make sure the box is away from bright lights, and out of the reach of cats, which prey on bats.

HELPFUL VISITORS

Bats **visit backyards to snack on small flying insects**, such as mosquitoes and flies. A small bat can eat up to 3,000 insects every night, making them great natural pest controllers.

Insect Feast

Anything that encourages insects to your backyard will also help to attract bats.

- Avoid using pesticides in your backyard.
- Plant flowers that bloom at night, such as evening primrose or moonflowers.

It's a Wrap!

Birthday parties are great fun, but cards, wrapping paper, and throwaway decorations can be an eco-disaster! Make sure your birthday doesn't cost the Earth by making these recycled decorations.

you will need

- used wrapping paper
- several yards of wool or string

tools

- scissors
- pen and ruler

USED WRAPPING PAPER

WOOL OR STRING

1. Work with one sheet of wrapping paper at a time. Start by snipping off any torn edges to make a large rectangle.

2. Fold the paper in half, widthways.

3. Use the ruler and pen to mark a line across the paper, around 2 inches from the fold.

2 in.

DON'T TRASH IT

Collect used wrapping paper for this project. You can also make the bunting using old plastic carrier bags. Cut the handles off and snip down the sides to make a large rectangle, then start from step 2.

4. Starting from the open end, cut the paper into strips, stopping when you get to the line.

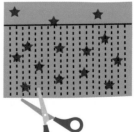

* The strips can be as wide or as narrow as you like—between 1/2 and 3/4 inch works well.

* When the party's over,
this bunting makes an
excellent bedroom decoration.

* Pause to
smooth out
the strips,
so they don't
get tangled.

5. Open the paper
out flat, and smooth
out the strips. Now
roll the paper
lengthwise, into a
long, thin sausage.

6. Pick up the
sausage and twist
the center tightly.

7. Fold the twist in
half and hold it in
place by twisting the
two sides together.

Party Time

Here are more ideas for a planet-friendly party:

- Old comics, maps,
or newspapers
make perfect
wrapping paper.
Finish with a bow
in a contrasting
color.

- Collect used cards
and cut out
pictures or shapes
to make your own
gift tags. Write
on the gift tag
instead of buying
a new card.

- Cut the torn
tops from used
envelopes,

decorate with
stickers, and turn
them into gift
bags for small
presents.

- Turn used cards
into brand-new
postcards by
cutting along
the fold.

- Don't buy special
party napkins—
cut a favorite
card into strips,
to make themed
napkin rings for
washable napkins.

* If the paper is too
thick to keep in place
with a twist, wrap a
piece of sticky tape
around the loop instead.

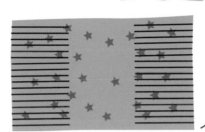

8. Use your fingers
to fluff up the strips.
Thread the decoration
onto a long piece of
wool or string.

9. Repeat steps 1 to 8 with
different sheets of paper, to
create brightly colored bunting
that flutters in the breeze!

Plant a Tree

An eco hero's secret weapons don't grow on trees... or do they? Learn how to clone plants from cuttings, and you can plant as many new trees as you like—one of the best ways to improve your local environment!

FLOWERPOT — THREE STICKS — COMPOST — SAND

you will need

- tall flowerpot with holes at the bottom
- sand
- compost
- large, clear plastic bag
- 3 sticks, each around twice the height of your pot
- rooting powder or liquid (optional)

tools

- sharp scissors (or garden shears)
- pencil
- gardening gloves
- watering can

Ask an Adult

1. Find a tree or shrub that you want to clone. Make sure you have permission from the owner of the land the tree is growing on. Find a shoot that has grown recently, and does not yet have flowers.

2. Cut off a long piece of newly grown shoot. Cut just above a pair of leaves or buds, so you don't damage the parent plant. Keep the cutting in a plastic bag until you are ready to pot it.

* Follow these steps to take a cutting in late spring or early summer. Shoots are ready for cutting if they snap when bent.

3. Wearing gloves, put a layer of sand at the bottom of the flowerpot. Fill the pot with compost. Press down firmly with your hand and water well.

— compost

— sand

TERRIFIC TREES

Trees are fantastic. A single large tree can provide food and shelter for thousands of different animals, from creepy-crawlies to birds and squirrels.

Trees also help to control the world's climate. As they grow, trees take in carbon dioxide from the air. The carbon is locked away in the roots, trunks, branches, and leaves, until the tree dies and rots (or is burned).

4. Use sharp scissors to trim the shoot, so it's 2 to 4 inches long. Make the cut just below a pair of leaves or buds.

5. Pull the lower leaves off the shoot (the ones that would be hidden by the soil).

* If there is a flower growing on the shoot, pinch it off.

* You can plant up to four cuttings in the same pot. In a few months, you'll have some to keep and some to give away.

* You can also dip the bottom of the cutting in rooting powder or liquid.

6. If any of the remaining leaves are very big, snip them in half. This will help encourage the shoot to grow new roots.

7. Make a hole in the compost with a pencil.

8. Push the shoot into the hole. Press the soil down around the shoot to fill the hole.

Change Champion

If you live in a town or city, trees are your secret weapons. Their roots help to hold soil together and control water flow, stopping flooding in heavy rain. They can hide ugly buildings and muffle the sound of traffic. They provide shade and mop up pollution from the air. They have even been shown to boost happiness! So get planting, and try to get your friends planting, too.

9. Push the sticks into the compost around the edge of the pot. Slide the bag over the sticks and pot, tucking the edges under the pot. This will help to keep the compost moist.

10. Put the covered pot in a warm, light place (but avoid direct sunlight). Keep the compost moist, and remove the bag every two weeks for ten minutes. When you do this, give the cutting a gentle tug. When it begins to pull the soil with it, you will know it has sprouted roots!

11. When your cutting has grown roots, remove the bag but keep the pot inside until the following autumn or spring.

12. Before you plant the cutting in the ground, put the pot outside for two weeks, to help the young tree get used to living outdoors. Then follow the steps in the box to plant your tree in its new home.

* Why not plant a tree every birthday, or to remember someone special?

26

How to Plant a Young Tree

- Choose the right time of year, when temperatures are not too hot or cold, and your tree will get enough rain. Autumn is good, as the tree can focus all its energy on growing roots rather than leaves or fruit.

- Choose a spot where the tree will have room to grow, at least 7 yards from other trees. Look at the parent plant to see how much room it might need. Don't plant a tree over pipes or under power lines. Get permission from the landowner first.

- Clear any leaves and grass to one side before digging a hole. You don't need to add anything to the soil, as tree roots will grow to find what they need. This helps anchor the tree in the soil.

- Make sure the hole is deep and wide enough that the roots won't be squashed together.

- Gently take the seedling out of the pot, along with its soil. Plant it quickly, so the roots don't dry out. The top root should be just below the surface of the soil.

- Fill the hole with loose soil, and gently push the soil around the tree to squeeze out any pockets of air. Water the tree with collected rainwater.

- If you plant the tree in dry weather, keep watering each week for as long as you can.

- Spreading rotting leaves or compost on the soil can help your new tree grow, but don't let this mulch touch the trunk.

Power Ranger

Gaps around windows and doors let warm air out, and chilly drafts in—brrrr! Instead of turning up the heat, turn on your eco-hero radar and zap the gaps. You can buy draft blockers in DIY stores, or make this no-sew version using socks!

you will need

- lots of old socks
- 2-yard length of string, wool, or elastic
- scraps of used plastic or fabric
- buttons (optional)

tools

- fabric scissors

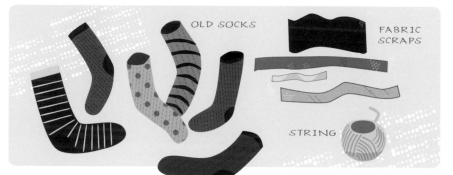

OLD SOCKS

FABRIC SCRAPS

STRING

* This is a great way to reuse mismatched or worn-out socks.

1. Turn a large sock inside out, and stuff a plastic bag (or scraps of fabric) into the toe.

2. Double up the string, wool, or elastic to make a one-yard length. Knot it around the sock to hold the plastic bag in place.

3. Fold the ankle over the rest of the sock to hide the knot.

4. Take a second sock, and snip off the toe to make a small hole.

* When you've finished, use buttons and fabric scraps to turn one end of the draft blocker into a friendly face.

* Save the scraps that you cut from the toes, and stuff them into the last sock (step 7).

DRAFT DETECTIVE

Draft-busting is one of the best ways to save energy in your home. Drafts make buildings feel colder than they really are, so zapping the gaps means you can turn down the heat and save money, too.

Use your draft blocker to fill gaps around doors and windows, attic hatches, and places where pipes lead outside. Don't block gaps that have been made on purpose to let in fresh air. These include bathroom and kitchen extractor fans, and vents in walls or windows.

5. Thread this sock onto the free end of the string. Push it snugly against the first sock.

6. Repeat steps 4 and 5 with the other socks. Make sure the socks are tightly packed. Stop adding socks when you are around 8 inches from the end of the string. Remember to save a sock for step 7!

7. Stuff a plastic bag (or fabric scraps) into the toe of a large sock. Knot the end of the string around this sock, to hold the others in place. Fold the ankle over to hide the knot.

8. Your draft blocker is ready to use. Bend it into the shape you need to zap that gap!

Action Grabber

Transform your trash into these great grabbers, so you can pick up litter without getting your hands dirty. They are so much fun to use, you'll be hunting for new places to tidy up!

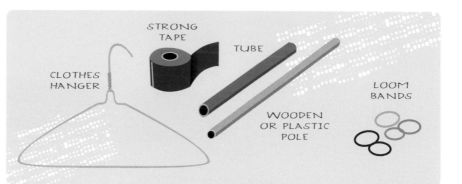

STRONG TAPE

TUBE

CLOTHES HANGER

WOODEN OR PLASTIC POLE

LOOM BANDS

you will need

- bendable wire clothes hanger
- strong tape
- 2-foot plastic or metal tube
- 3-foot wooden or plastic pole that fits inside the pipe—make sure it's not too snug!
- old loom bands or rubber bands

tools

- gardening gloves

* Wear gardening gloves while you bend the clothes hanger, so your hands don't get hurt.

1. Grab the hook of the clothes hanger and carefully straighten it out.

Ask an Adult

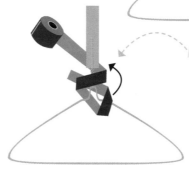

2. Line up the straightened wire with the bottom of the pole, and tape them together. Use plenty of tape, wrapping it through the hanger to make the connection super strong.

3. Grab the sides of the hanger (the parts that fit in the shoulders) and bend them together until they touch. They should spring apart a little when you release them. These are the "fingers" of your grabber.

Change Champion

You probably know that litter pollutes the environment and harms wildlife. But did you know that $11.5 billion a year is spent on cleaning up litter in the United States alone? What a waste! The best way to reduce littering in your local streets and parks is to reduce what you need to throw away. Reuse water bottles instead of buying a fresh one. Carry food in a washable container instead of buying wrapped snacks. If you have to get rid of trash, carry it with you until you find a bin—ideally a recycling bin! And save your best scowl for anyone who doesn't do the same.

USING JUNK

Look out for junk that you can recycle to make the grabber. You could use a spare piece of piping from a plumbing project (aim for between 1 and 1 1/4 inches in diameter). An old broom handle or length of bamboo makes a perfect pole. Clothes shops can often reuse clothes hangers, but this is a good way to recycle flimsy ones.

5. Push the free end of the pole through the tube until it sticks out of the other end.

6. Your grabber is now ready to use. Hold the top of the pipe with one hand, and pull on the pole with the other. The fingers will pinch together to pick up litter. To drop the litter, hold it over a bin or trashcan and push the pole back into the pipe.

4. Stretch some loom bands or rubber bands around each finger, for grip.

* The grabber helps you reach into bushes and long grass without getting hurt.

Upcycling

Upcycling means reinventing a worn-out household object or piece of furniture. Instead of throwing away the tiny tables and chairs you used as a kid, use this trick to turn them into furniture that you can read!

you will need

- old piece of furniture
- sandpaper
- PVA glue
- water
- old comics or magazines

tools

- paintbrush
- sanding block (optional)

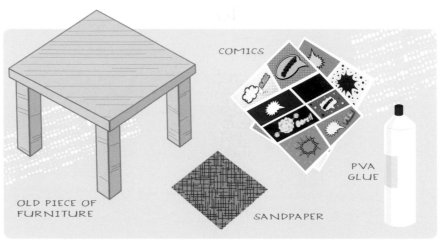

COMICS

PVA GLUE

OLD PIECE OF FURNITURE

SANDPAPER

Change Champion

It's always better to reuse objects than to buy new. The bigger the object, the bigger the eco-hero impact! If you do have to get rid of furniture, sell it or give it away locally, or donate it to a charity—some specialize in secondhand furniture. Visit these stores to grab a bargain yourself.

1. Sand the table down to remove any big lumps or bumps. Wipe the dust off with a wet cloth.

* **Wear a dust mask when sanding.**

2. Cut or tear the comics into pieces. Will you go straight and neat or shabby chic?

3. Squeeze three tablespoons of PVA glue into a jar or bowl. Add a tablespoon of water and mix well.

SPREAD THE WORD

The process of layering paper to cover a surface has a fancy craft name—découpage. It's a great way to reuse old comics and magazines and personalize your bedroom—whether you're into superheroes, sports, or ponies!

This is the fun part!

4. Dunk your paintbrush into the glue and spread a thin layer of glue on a small area of the table you are decorating. Lay a piece of comic on top, and use the paintbrush to smooth it out and squeeze out any air bubbles.

5. Add the next piece of comic in the same way, overlapping the edges. Repeat until the whole table is covered.

6. Brush a coat of watered-down PVA glue across the whole table. Let it dry overnight and then repeat.

Get Sticking!

Use this trick to revamp smaller objects and make great gifts. Try it on:

- old mirrors and picture frames
- desks and box files
- a bashed or boring set of shelves
- the fronts or insides of drawers (your socks have never had so much fun!).

* This will give your design a tough, waterproof finish.

Hidden Hero

Bird watching is a great way to discover more about the wildlife on your doorstep. You'll see more if the birds don't know you're there—and that's where this handy hide comes in!

you will need

- 5-foot garden cane (or stick)
- Two 2-foot pieces of garden cane (or sticks)
- wire or twine
- 7 x 7-foot sheet of green/brown fabric or netting
- clothespins

tools

- scissors

STICKS

FABRIC

WIRE OR TWINE

CLOTHESPINS

DATA LOG

Keep a record of the birds that you spot in your yard and other places. At certain times of year, national organizations collect data from bird watchers like you. They use it to help track bird populations and find out which species are threatened.

1. Use wire or twine to tie the short sticks together at one end, at right angles.

2. Stand the sticks up to make a triangle. Use the wire or twine to join the long stick at one end. The frame should now stand up on its own.

3. Lay the sheet of fabric out in the place where you will be watching birds. Place the frame on top of the sheet at one side.

4. Pick up the other side of the sheet, and carefully wrap it around the frame. Use clothespins to clip the sheet to the frame.

5. Camouflage the sheet with any fallen leaves and branches that you can find nearby. Using found materials will help to convince birds that the hide is part of the landscape!

6. Fold the end of the sheet back over the highest point of the frame. Cut a small rectangle at eye level.

7. When you are ready to begin birdwatching, crawl backward into the hide. Flap the front of the hide up, and aim your eyes, camera, or binoculars through the hole!

* Tempt birds to land nearby by putting out food in winter months, or nest-building materials in spring. Try a collection of small twigs, moss, dried leaves, and dried grass.

What Can I Do to Help Birds?

Here are some ways to encourage birds to visit your yard:

- Put out food in cold weather (see page 50).
- Encourage insects to live in your yard (see page 42 and 52), so birds have plenty to eat in warm weather.
- Put stickers in windows, to stop birds from flying into the glass.
- Build a birdbath or mini pond (see page 6), to give birds somewhere to drink and bathe.
- Keep pet cats indoors.
- Don't use pesticides in your yard.
- Never disturb a bird's nest.
- Close curtains before you put lights on at night.

Ride to the Rescue

Cut back on short car journeys by cycling instead. This tough, waterproof pouch is the perfect place to stash your stuff on two wheels.

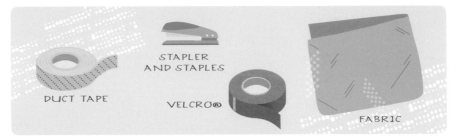

DUCT TAPE

STAPLER AND STAPLES

VELCRO®

FABRIC

you will need

- tough, waterproof fabric
- stapler and staples
- duct tape
- 1½ in. Velcro®

tools

- scissors
- ruler and pen

* An old rain jacket or tough, reusable carrier bag would be perfect for this project. Brightly colored fabric helps to make you more visible on the road.

1. Cut a rectangle of fabric, roughly 2 feet x 1 foot big. Lay it on a flat surface with the "right" side facing up.

2. Imagine a line about a quarter of the way down the fabric. Fold up the bottom of the fabric to meet this line.

* The "right" side is the side that you would like to see on the outside of your finished pouch.

6 in.

9 in.

3. Punch a neat line of staples along one side, to hold the two layers of fabric together. Place the staples very close together. Repeat on the other side.

GO BY BIKE

Cars release greenhouse gases and other pollutants. Replacing short car trips with walking or cycling is one of the best ways to clean up your local environment.

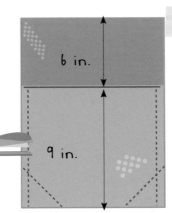

4. Punch a line of staples across each of the bottom corners, to make a triangle.

* Tape over the edges to make them extra strong.

5. Fold the top, front edge of the pouch down, and use a neat line of staples to hold it in place.

6. Use the ruler and pen to divide the top flap into five rectangles. Cut away the rectangle at each side and cut along the other lines, leaving three straps. Use a damp cloth to wipe off any pen marks.

7. Carefully turn the pouch inside out.

8. Pull the right-hand strap out, with the "right" side face down. Fold the corners inward to make a triangle. Cut a piece of Velcro® 1 inch long, and staple the fuzzy side onto the triangle. Do the same for the left-hand strap.

9. Staple the spiky piece of Velcro® at the base of the right-hand strap. Do the same for the left-hand strap.

10. Repeat step 8 for the middle strap, but staple the matching piece of Velcro® to the front of the pouch.

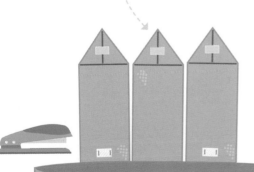

11. Attach the pouch to your bike by wrapping the straps around the handlebar, using the Velcro® to hold them in place.

* Pack a water bottle and bicycle pump, for easy-breezy cycling!

37

Kitchen Wizard

Humans throw away millions of tons of food and drink every year. Zapping this waste would be as good for the planet as taking a quarter of our cars off the road! Start with this cunning plan for saving bruised or overripe fruit from the trash.

you will need

FOR THE TOFFEE FRUIT MIX:

- overripe fruit such as bananas, pears, and apples
- one tablespoon of sugar for every cup of fruit
- one tablespoon of butter for every cup of fruit

FOR THE PANCAKES (MAKES 4):

- ½ cup plain flour
- one egg
- one cup milk
- one tablespoon of butter

utensils

- ovenproof dish
- large bowl
- whisk
- fork or potato masher
- frying pan
- ladle

SUGAR

FLOUR

EGG

MIXED FRUIT

BUTTER

MILK

1. Ask an adult to help you cut the fruit into chunks.

Ask an Adult

2. Put the fruit into an ovenproof dish, and sprinkle with the sugar and dabs of butter.

3. Ask an adult to pop the dish in an oven heated to 350°F for about 20 minutes, until it's sticky and bubbling.

4. When the fruit is cooked, bring it out of the oven and mash it with a fork or masher. While the fruit cools, make the pancakes.

Too Good to Waste!

Half the food we throw away could still be eaten. Instead, it ends up in landfills, where it rots and produces greenhouse gases. Here's how to stop the rot:

- Use food before it goes bad. This will reduce the amount of food that you need to buy, saving water, energy, and other resources.
- Buy fruit and vegetables even if they don't look perfect. If they are in the shop, they are safe to eat.
- If you can't eat it, compost it! Composting reduces methane emissions, recycles nutrients, and makes you notice how much food is being wasted.
- Use a similar trick with limp vegetables. Chop and roast in the oven, then blend or mash to make a delicious pasta sauce.
- Overripe fruit can be used to make all sorts of yummy treats, from jam and smoothies, to cake and crumble!

5. Whisk the flour, egg, and milk together until all the lumps have disappeared.

* If you have spare baked fruit, freeze it and reheat it next time you are in the mood for pancakes! It's also yummy with ice cream or yogurt.

6. Ask an adult to help you melt the butter in a frying pan. Stir the melted butter into the pancake mix, leaving a thin film of butter in the pan.

7. Add a ladleful of batter to the pan and cook the pancake on each side until golden.

8. Serve the pancakes with your sticky toffee fruit topping!

* Pancakes are a great way to use up eggs and milk that are about to spoil.

Save the Salad

Bagged salads and herbs are some of the most commonly wasted foods. Banish the bags by growing your own salads and herbs the easy way—in pots that water themselves!

you will need

- large plastic drink bottle, washed and dried
- compost
- old cotton T-shirt or leggings
- acrylic paints

tools

- scissors

DRINK BOTTLE

ACRYLIC PAINTS

OLD T-SHIRT OR LEGGINGS

COMPOST

NO BAGS!

Most supermarket salads and herbs are sold in bags, so we may buy more than we need. Tucked away in the fridge, they quickly turn brown and slimy—explaining why more than two-thirds of bagged leaves end up in the trash. Growing your own salads and herbs will help your family cut down on food waste.

1. Carefully cut the bottle in half, saving both pieces. Remove the lid.

Ask an Adult

2. The bottom half will become a water reservoir. Draw a fun outline, such as animal ears, and carefully trim around it.

3. Decorate the reservoir with paints. When the paint has dried, half-fill the reservoir with water.

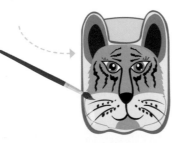

1 ft.

1 in.

4. Cut three strips from the old cotton T-shirt. Each strip should be 1 inch wide and 1 foot long.

* Save the rest of the cotton for the projects on page 58!

Top Tips for Zapping Food Waste

- Keep cut herbs fresh by storing them in a glass of water in the fridge door.

- If you spot bagged herbs looking limp, or cut too much from your own plants, just wash, chop, and freeze until they are needed.

- Most other foods, including bread and cakes, can be frozen right up to their "use by" date. Even opened jars of food can be frozen! Almost a quarter of wasted food is thrown away too early, because people don't understand food labels.

- Use clips or jars to stop open packets of food from drying out.

5. Plait the strips and tie a knot at each end.

6. Feed the plaited fabric through the neck of the top half of your bottle.

* Keep store-bought pots of herbs alive longer by transplanting them into a self-watering pot.

7. Hold the fabric in place while you fill the top half of the bottle with compost.

* These self-watering planters make great gifts. Paint the reservoir with a design that will look funny with herb "hair"!

8. Place the top half of the bottle on top of the reservoir, so the end of the plait sits in the water. Water will be drawn up through the fabric, into the pot. All you need to do is top off the reservoir every few weeks.

Backyard Jungle

There's just one rule for creating a wildlife-friendly yard—the messier the better! Turn a small patch of lawn into a mini wildflower meadow, to bring bees, butterflies, birds, and bats to your backyard.

CARDBOARD

WILDFLOWER SEEDS

CRAYON

you will need

- large piece of cardboard
- 2 g of wildflower seeds

tools

- crayon and scissors
- spade and rake
- watering can

* Start this project in autumn or early spring.

1. Fold a large piece of cardboard in half. Draw half a butterfly along the fold.

2. Cut around the shape and open out to make a large butterfly template. Lay the template on the area of lawn that you would like to transform.

3. Push the spade into the ground to mark around the template.

Change Champion

Neat lawns and weeded flowerbeds are bad for wildlife. Insects need weeds for food and shelter. Letting part of your yard go "wild" is the best way to help insects. You'll be more likely to spot birds and bats, too, because they snack on creepy-crawlies. Your boring yard can be transformed into an eco-friendly jungle!

4. Dig out the grass inside the butterfly shape, until you have a hole around 6-8 inches deep. Keep as much of the soil as possible, but throw the grass and all the roots onto the compost heap.

5. Break up the soil, firm it down again, and rake it level. You don't need to add anything to the soil—wildflowers grow best on "bad" soil.

6. Scatter wildflower seeds all over the butterfly shape.

7. Rake gently to cover the seeds with a thin layer of soil, then water them well.

8. Water the patch regularly until seedlings appear.

9. When the seeds begin to germinate, you'll have a beautiful butterfly garden that keeps changing color. Why not make other insect shapes, too?

BEES PLEASE!

Most land that was once covered in wildflowers is now farmland, growing just one type of crop or grass. This is bad news for insects, and bad news for humans. As they visit flowers looking for food, insects do a very important job—pollination. Without pollination, plants don't produce seeds and fruit. We rely on insects such as bees to pollinate almost three-quarters of the crops we eat!

* Always wash your hands after touching soil.

* Use a mix of wildflower seeds. Different wildflowers will flower at different times, feeding insects from April to October.

Where to Plant

Make sure you ask the owner of the lawn before you start. If they say no, try one of these ideas instead:

- Let part of a lawn grow longer, so that plants such as clover can flower.
- Plant wildflowers in a container.
- Plant wildflowers on a patch of "wasteland," along a driveway or sidewalk.
- Ask your teacher if you can plant a wildflower garden at school.

Basket Weaver

Most packaging is made of plastic and cardboard, two of the most difficult and expensive materials to recycle. They often end up being burned or buried as landfill. Keep packaging out of the trash by giving it a second life as sassy storage!

THICK CARD

STICKY TAPE

ELASTIC BANDS

OLD PACKAGING

you will need

- old packaging material, the brighter the better
- sticky tape
- long elastic bands
- piece of thick card
- stapler (optional)

tools

- scissors
- bucket, box, or bowl

* The length of your longest strips will determine the size of basket you can make. If you only have short strips, try using a small bowl or even a cardboard tube as a support instead of a bucket.

1. Cut the packaging material into long strips, 1/2-3/4 inch wide.

↕ 1/2-3/4 in.

2. Turn the bucket upside down. Take two of your longest strips, and cross them over on top of the bucket. Use a small piece of tape to hold them to each other (but not the bucket).

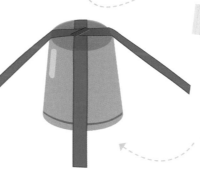

3. Add more strips to fill the gaps, using a little tape to stick each one to the strip below.

4. Bend the strips around the bucket, and hold them in place with the elastic bands.

5. Take a new strip of packaging material, and tape it to one of the strips, near the base of the bucket.

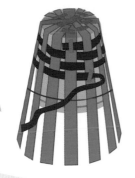

6. Weave this strip in and out of the vertical strips, working your way around the bucket. When you come to the end of the first strip, simply tape it to a new strip and keep weaving!

7. Work your way down the bucket in the same way, until you get to the bottom (or run out of strips).

8. Turn the bucket the right way up. Trim the vertical strips so that they stick up around 1 inch above the topmost horizontal strip.

9. Carefully remove the elastic bands. Slip the bucket out of the basket.

10. Fold each vertical strip over the topmost horizontal strip, securing them with sticky tape or staples.

* Some strips will be folded inward, and others outward, to hold the topmost horizontal strip in place.

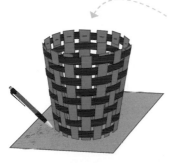

11. Draw around the base of the bucket on a scrap of thick card. Cut out the shape, and slot it into the bottom of your basket.

THE PROBLEM WITH PLASTIC

Plastic is a popular packaging material because it is tough, waterproof, and doesn't get broken down by bacteria and fungi. Once the packaging has been used, these pros turn into cons—plastics buried in landfill sites don't biodegrade, and will take hundreds of years to break down. Be an eco hero by buying products with less packaging, and finding ways to keep plastic out of the trash.

Shower Power

you will need

- 2 small identical plastic bottles or jars, cleaned and dried
- fine sand
- piece of shiny junk mail, or a shiny magazine cover
- PVC tape
- suction cup with hook (optional)

tools

- hole punch
- stopwatch or clock with a second hand
- scissors

Showers save water and energy compared to baths— but only if they are short. This recycled sand timer is your secret weapon.

TWO BOTTLES

SAND

JUNK MAIL

PVC TAPE

1. Cut a small circle from the junk mail. Fold it into quarters. Snip the point off, then open it up to make a simple funnel.

2. Use the funnel to fill the first bottle with sand.

3. Cut a new piece of the junk mail, twice as wide as the opening of your jar or bottle. Punch a hole in the center.

* Pet stores, toy shops, or craft stores may stock fine sand. Colored sand would work well.

BOTTLE BANK

This project is a neat way to recycle small glass or plastic containers, such as food coloring bottles or spice jars. Clean and dry the containers thoroughly, as wet sand will not flow.

4. Tape the paper with the hole over the neck of the bottle or jar full of sand.

5. Start timing as you turn the bottle over and let the sand run out into an empty bowl or dish. When four minutes have passed, put your thumb over the hole to stop more sand from flowing out. Discard the rest of the sand from the bottle.

6. Fill the second bottle or jar with the sand you collected in the bowl.

7. Tape the bottles or jar together very firmly at the neck, so no paper is showing.

8. To hang your sand timer in the shower, tape a loop of old plastic packaging to each end.

9. Use a suction cup with a hook to hang your timer in the shower. Simply turn it over to start the four-minute countdown!

Change Champion

Showers pump out a quarter of all the water we use in our homes. The average shower is 8 minutes long, using 16 to 18 gallons of water—almost enough to fill a bath! Power showers may use more water than a bath. Cutting daily showers down to 4 minutes can help a family of four save about 13,000 gallons of water every year—enough to fill an articulated tanker truck. You'll also save money on heating the water. So, ask everyone in the house to use your sand timer!

* If the sand flows too quickly, try punching a smaller hole in the paper. Experiment with the materials you have to get a 4-minute flow.

Bird Hero

Birds need eco heroes on their side in the cold winter months, when it's much harder for them to find food. Make this hanging feeder and stock it with homemade bird cakes to provide a big energy boost for your feathered friends.

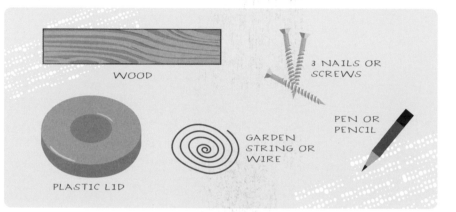

WOOD

3 NAILS OR SCREWS

PEN OR PENCIL

PLASTIC LID

GARDEN STRING OR WIRE

you will need

- 10-inch length of wood, at least 1 inch thick
- old pen or pencil
- 3 nails or self-tapping screws
- large, clean plastic lid, e.g., from a tub of ice cream or paint
- PVA glue (optional)
- garden string or wire

tools

- ruler and pen
- saw and sandpaper
- hammer and screwdriver
- hand drill (or adult with a power drill)

* Look out for chunky pieces of wood that you can upcycle, such as an old chair leg or table leg.

1. Saw your length of wood down to about 10 inches, and sand off any paint or varnish.

Ask an adult

2. Mark a point in the center of the wood, about a quarter of the way up from the bottom.

10 in.

* Put a piece of old wood underneath to protect the surface you are working on.

3. Use a hand drill with a drill bit the same diameter as your pencil (or slightly larger). Drill all the way through the wood at the marked point.

2.5 in.

4. Sand around the hole on both sides, for a smooth finish.

10 in.

3 in.

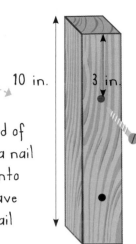

5. Mark a second point at the center of the wood, about a third of the way from the top. Hammer a nail (or drive a self-tapping screw) into the wood at that point—but leave about 3/4 inch of the screw or nail sticking out of the wood.

6. Repeat step 5 on the other side of the wood, but a bit lower.

7. Make four holes around the edges of the plastic roof.

8. Push the pencil through the large drilled hole, so it sticks out on both sides.

9. Use the third nail or screw to fix the center of the plastic lid to the top of the wood. This will be the roof of your feeder.

10. Feed garden string or wire through the holes in the lid, and tie knots to make loops for hanging.

* If the pencil is not a tight fit, dab a little PVA glue inside the hole to hold it in place.

WHEN TO FEED BIRDS

Feeding birds isn't just a good way to bring wildlife to your yard. It can help birds to survive a cold winter. Wild birds normally eat a mixture of insects, earthworms, larvae, fruits, and berries, but these things are much harder to find in winter. Fatty foods such as seeds, nuts, and lard cakes give birds the extra energy they need. In spring and summer, put out sunflower seeds, raisins, and soft fruits instead of the lard cakes on the next page.

........Now it's time to make the bird food!

ORANGE   LARD   SEED MIX

1. Put the lard into a mixing bowl. Stand the bowl in warm water until the lard is soft and gooey.

2. Add the seed mix, and stir.

* If you want to add a special treat, try dried fruit or grated cheese!

you will need

- one orange, cut in half
- half a block of lard
- 2 handfuls of seed mix for wild birds

utensils

- mixing bowl
- spoon

3. Use the spoon to scoop the soft flesh from each half of the orange. You can eat this (yum!) but wash your hands first, if you have been touching birdseed.

4. Wash and dry the orange halves, then scoop half of the lard and seed mix into each one.

5. Turn each orange half over and poke a small hole in the skin.

6. Use the holes to hook the bird cakes onto the nail or screw on each side of your feeder. Your bird buffet is open for business!

* If you have spare mixture, fill more orange halves, sandwich them together, and store in a food bag in the freezer. You can also freeze the mix in an old container. Make sure you label it as bird food.

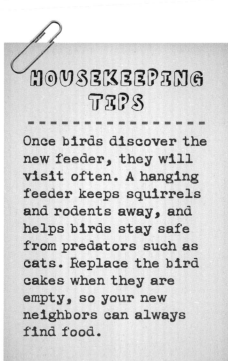

HOUSEKEEPING TIPS

Once birds discover the new feeder, they will **visit** often. A hanging feeder keeps squirrels and rodents away, and helps birds stay safe from predators such as cats. Replace the bird cakes when they are empty, so your new neighbors can always find food.

Bird Hero Dos and Don'ts

Follow these tips to make sure you help and don't harm birds:

- Do use a mixture of seeds to attract different types of birds to your garden, yard, or balcony.

- Don't put out fat balls in a net. Nets can trap birds' feet and beaks.

- Do stick to suet or lard for homemade bird cakes. Cooking fat or soft spreads can harm birds.

- Don't forget to put out a dish of water, too!

- Do clean your feeder. It won't get covered in droppings like a bird table, but move it around once a month so droppings don't build up on the ground.

- Don't put fat cakes out in spring and summer. Birds don't need as much extra food when it's warm, and fat can actually harm baby birds. Instead, try sticking a soft apple, banana, or pear on your feeder.

- Do wash your hands after cleaning or restocking your bird feeder.

Bugtropolis

Build a minibeast apartment block and attract a host of helpful insects to your garden, such as ladybugs, bees, and beetles.

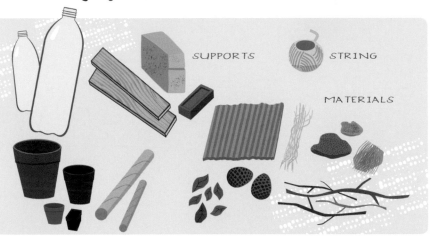

you will need

- old bricks and large stones
- wooden planks
- supports such as old flowerpots, plastic bottles, pots, pipes or tubes, blocks of untreated wood
- materials such as cardboard, straw, hay, pinecones, dead twigs and branches, dried leaves, moss

tools

- scissors
- secateurs
- hacksaw
- string

SUPPORTS   STRING

MATERIALS

1. Begin by building a simple structure. Choose a sheltered wall or fence that doesn't get too much sun. Stack bricks and planks to create a stepped structure that rests against the wall.

* Vary the height and depth of each layer, to attract creatures of different sizes.

HIDING PLACES

Have you ever found creepy-crawlies hiding under a stone or log in the garden? Insects and other bugs seek out safe nooks and crannies to lay eggs and shelter in cold weather. If you don't have natural habitats such as log piles in your garden, build an artificial "apartment block" out of natural and recycled objects.

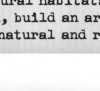

2. Prepare different "apartments" for your bug building by stuffing containers with different natural and recycled materials.

Change Champion

Bugtropolis provides shelter for many different creepy-crawlies. Spread the word—each one is a garden hero in its own way. Bees, butterflies, and many flies are pollinators (see page 43). Ladybugs, lacewings, spiders, and wasps (or their larvae) chomp on smaller insects that damage plants. This natural pest control means you don't need to use pesticides in your garden. Woodlice, earwigs, and beetles feed on dead and decaying material in the garden, returning nutrients to the soil in their droppings!

Try out some of these ideas, or be creative with the materials you have at hand.

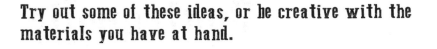

- Cut a large branch into sections, and ask an adult to drill some holes in one end.

Ask an Adult

- Roll up a strip of cardboard, and stuff it into a waterproof container.

- Collect moss from the tops of walls, or look out for clumps dropped by birds in spring.

- Cut bamboo canes or twigs into short pieces.

- Collect dried leaves from flowerbeds.

- Chop up branches and twigs so they are roughly the same length, and pack them inside an old cardboard tube.

- Collect dead bark from fallen trees.

- Tie bundles of twigs together with garden string.

3. Have fun fitting the different apartments into the Bugtropolis structure. Try to pack the materials together tightly, so they don't blow away in the wind.

* Your insects will also need food and drink, so why not plant a wildflower jungle (see page 42) and a mini pond (see page 6) nearby!

Dry leaves and bark will attract beetles, woodlice, and spiders.

Some bees like to lay eggs in narrow tubes or holes. If you spot a tube that has been sealed with mud or leaves, you'll know it's occupied!

Lacewings can shelter inside tightly rolled cardboard.

Ladybugs like to roost among dry sticks and leaves.

Centipedes and earwigs will feel at home in a log pile.

Comic Book Farmer

Eco heroes eat locally grown food, and you can't get more local than your backyard! You don't need a lot of land or special tools to grow fruits and vegetables. Take an old comic and a waterproof tray, and start an eco-friendly farm on your windowsill.

you will need

- old comic or magazine
- waterproof tray or dish
- seed-growing compost
- fruit or vegetable seeds, such as tomato, carrot, sweetcorn, peas, or broad beans
- clingfilm

tools

- pencil

* Don't use shiny magazine covers for this project. They are coated with plastic and will not biodegrade when you plant them.

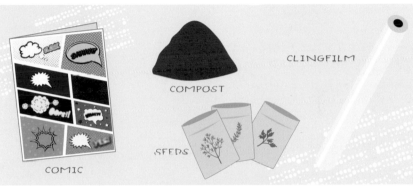

COMIC   COMPOST   SEEDS   CLINGFILM

1. Take one comic page and fold the short edges together.

2. Fold the paper in half again, and open out to leave a crease at the center.

3. With the fold nearest to you, fold each corner to the center crease to make a triangle (as if you were making a paper boat).

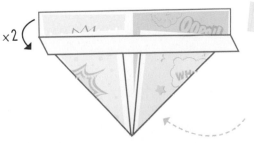

×2

4. Take the upper layer of the top flap, and fold it down to meet the base of the triangle. Fold down again, to hide the base of the triangle.

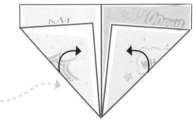

5. Turn the paper over. Fold each side in to meet the center crease.

×2

6. Repeat step 4, folding the flap down twice. You will have made a little pocket.

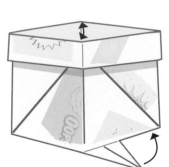

7. Fold the point up to meet the bottom of the flap, crease, and unfold.

8. Open the pocket up while pushing the bottom point toward one of the corners. It will fold under to make a flat base.

9. Press your fingers inside the pot to flatten the base.

10. Repeat steps 1 to 9 to make as many pots as you need! Put your pots into a waterproof tray, and fill them with seed-growing compost. Give the compost a light sprinkle of water.

11. Plant two or three seeds in each pot, following the instructions on the packets.

* Use a pencil to make a hole for each seed.

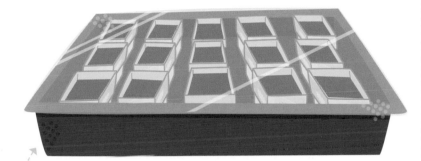

Change Champion

Transporting food from farm, to factory, to warehouse, to shop, to homes uses energy. In the United States, fruits and vegetables travel an average of 1,500 miles from the farm where they were grown before they get to a plate. Growing some of your own fruits and vegetables reduces the food miles for each meal. You can also make sure homegrown produce is organic (grown without artificial chemicals, such as fertilizers and pesticides). This is kinder to wildlife and the environment.

12. Cover the whole tray with clingfilm, and put it in a warm place. Make sure the compost stays moist but not too damp by watering the tray, not the seeds! Try not to let the paper dry out.

* If you are planting several types of seeds at once, write the name of the seed in each pot directly onto the paper using a waterproof marker.

* If any paper shows above ground, it will draw water away from the plant's roots.

13. When shoots and leaves appear, remove the clingfilm and move the tray to a sunny place. Remove the smallest, weakest shoots in each pot, to give the strongest plant more space to grow.

14. When it's almost time to plant the seedlings outside, dig holes a little deeper than each pot. Plant the whole pot, making sure the paper is completely covered with soil. The roots will grow through the paper.

Rip It Up!

Cut out clothes waste by donating outgrown garments to friends, family, or charity shops. Even worn-out clothes can be turned into something you do want to keep—like this colorful rag rug.

OLD T-SHIRTS

1. Lay a T-shirt flat on the floor, and cut across the bottom to make a loop of fabric, around 1 inch wide.

1 in.

2. Slip the loop around two legs of a small table. It should be tightly stretched. If it isn't tight, cut the loop and retie it.

1 in.

4. Cut the remaining cotton clothes into long strips, about 1 inch wide. Knot the strips together to make one long strip.

3. Repeat steps 1 and 2 until there are 8 to 10 loops of fabric between the table legs.

FABULOUS FABRICS

A lot of our clothes are made from cotton, but this fabric is not very eco friendly (see page 13). Organic cotton is grown without chemicals and it is a better choice, but these clothes can be expensive and hard to find. However, there are other natural fibers that can be used for making clothes—and these are kinder to the planet. Hemp, bamboo, and soya plants can all be turned into fabric, though some methods of doing it are more sustainable than others. Reusing clothes is still the best bet!

5. Knot the end of the long strip onto the bottom loop, at the left-hand side.

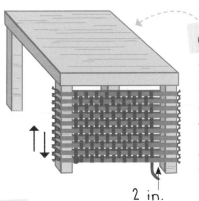

6. Working from bottom to top, weave the long strip of fabric loosely over and under the loops of fabric on the table. When you get to the top, change direction and weave back down to the bottom.

2 in.

7. Keep weaving until you are about 2 inches from the right-hand table leg. If you run out of fabric on the way, simply knot on another strip.

* On the way back down, pass the fabric over the strips you went under last time.

8. Knot the end of the long strip of fabric to one of the loops. Now carefully snip each end of the loops to remove the rug from the table.

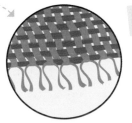

9. Knot the loose ends together in pairs to finish your rug!

Change Champion

Change Champion

the Bag It Up project (page 13) looked at why it is important to reuse and recycle fabrics, but it's also important to spread the word to your friends and family. Giving them a handmade, upcycled fabric present such as the rug or bags in this book will show them how old fabrics can be given a new purpose! If you want to make more fabric projects but you need extra supplies, ask your friends and family to donate their worn-out clothes to you.

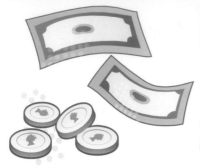

Start a Shop

You'll need help to save the planet, so it's time to spread the word to your friends, family, and neighbors. One way to do this is to run a pop-up shop in your community, selling your eco-crafts or services.

you will need

- an adult to help
- lots of ideas
- a venue for your stall

IDEAS   ADULT

What to Sell

This book is packed with projects that you can scale up and sell:

- Get cooking—turn a glut of seasonal fruit into sweet treats (page 38).
- Run an arts and crafts stall selling cloth bags (page 10), draft excluders (page 28), upcycled objects (page 32), or self-watering plant pots (page 40).

- Grow new plants from cuttings or seeds (page 24), and sell them when they are ready to plant outside in spring or summer.
- Make bird feeders and bird food (page 48–51) to sell in winter.

1. Start by deciding what to sell. Some of the upcycled crafts in this book make great gifts that people may be willing to buy. Try teaming up with friends to make as much stock as possible. You will be raising money from trash!

2. Ask an adult to help you pick a date, time, and place for your shop. You will need an adult with you on the day.

* If you want to run a stall selling food, check the health and safety regulations in your area.

Have you heard the buzz?

Come and buy bee-friendly plants for your yard!

• Eco-Hero Primary School
• Honeybee Lane
• March 1 at 2pm

Save our bees and save the planet!

Raising money for our school garden

3. Find eco-friendly ways to advertise your event. Make posters from scrap paper and display them at local shops, schools, libraries, and businesses. Remember to include:

• date, time, and place

• what will be on offer

• what you are raising money for.

4. Borrow tables and chairs. Ask an adult to loan you some money so that you can give people change.

5. On the day, get there in plenty of time to set up. Make your stall look attractive, so people want to visit. Welcome customers with a big smile and have your best eco-hero tips at hand.

Swap Shop

Ask your school or community group if they would like to run an event to raise funds for bigger eco-projects. You don't have to bake or make anything. Try running an "as new" stall, selling (or just swapping) unwanted belongings. Encourage people to come by asking local businesses to sponsor a fashion show, where "old" clothes are styled to suit the latest trends. Alternatively, you could auction off eco-friendly services, such as digging a mini pond, building a bug hotel, or planting a tree. Remember— you will need the help and permission of an adult before setting up an event or stall of any kind.

* Put up a big sign so people know what you are selling.

Have you heard the buzz?

Save our bees and save the planet!

Raising money for our school garden

Web Warrior

Eco heroes are always looking for more ways to save the planet. Start with these websites. They are great places to go for more information and ideas.

WILDLIFE WARRIOR

ic.fsc.org
Get your school involved in protecting wildlife with the Forestry Stewardship Council website.

www.foei.org
Friends of the Earth work to protect nature. Get involved in their latest campaigns.

www.ams.usda.gov/AMSv1.0/NOPFactSheets
This United States Department of Agriculture (USDA) site provides fact sheets about organic food and farming.

WASTE ZAPPER

www.nclnet.org/understanding_sell_by_dates
This site will help you to understand food labels, so you don't throw anything away too soon.

satruck.org
Put old furniture to good use by donating it to the Salvation Army.

www.epa.gov/recycle
The Environmental Protection Agency (EPA) website is great for finding out more about reducing, reusing, and recycling.

GREEN MACHINE

www.nature.org/greenliving/carboncalculator/
Visit this website to calculate your family's carbon footprint, and find out how to reduce it.

energy.gov/public-services
Find out how to save energy every day in your home.

www.kab.org/site/PageServer?pagename=litterprevention_what_you_can_do
Find out how to get involved with initiatives to stop littering and clean up the environment.

Glossary

biodegradable rots away naturally

carbon dioxide a gas that is breathed out by plants and animals, and also released when fossil fuels are burned; a greenhouse gas

carbon footprint the amount of carbon dioxide released into the atmosphere by a person or a group of people

climate the usual weather conditions in an area

compost rotten plant and animal matter, used to help new plants grow

draft a cool breeze in a room

energy efficient uses as little energy as possible

environment the place in which a person, plant, or animal lives

environmentally friendly does not harm the environment

food miles the distance that food (or each ingredient in food) has been transported, from producer to plate

food waste when food is produced, but thrown away instead of being eaten

germinated began to grow from a seed

global warming the warming of Earth's climate, due to the greenhouse effect

greenhouse gases gases that trap heat from the Sun when they build up in the atmosphere

hibernate spend winter in a deep sleep

landfill getting rid of trash by burying it in large pits

larva a young insect

methane a gas that is burped out by cows and other animals; one of the main greenhouse gases

microbes tiny living things that can only be seen with a microscope, such as bacteria

organic grown in a way that is friendly to the environment and wildlife, without using artificial chemicals, such as fertilizers

pesticide chemical used to kill pests, such as insects that eat crops

pollination transferring pollen from one flower to another, which allows seeds to form

pollute contaminate something with harmful substances or objects

pollution when harmful substances are introduced into the environment

recycle change trash or waste into something new

reuse use something again

suet a type of animal fat, used in cooking

wildlife the animals and plants that live in an area

Index